BAKE YOUR OWN
COOKIES

BY MARI BOLTE

PEBBLE
a capstone imprint

Published by Pebble, an imprint of Capstone
1710 Roe Crest Drive, North Mankato, Minnesota 56003
capstonepub.com

Copyright © 2026 by Capstone. All rights reserved. No part of this publication may be reproduced in whole or in part, or stored in a retrieval system, or transmitted in any form or by any means, electronic, mechanical, photocopying, recording, or otherwise, without written permission of the publisher.

Library of Congress Cataloging-in-Publication Data
Names: Bolte, Mari, author.
Title: Bake your own cookies / by Mari Bolte.
Description: North Mankato, Minnesota : Pebble, an imprint of Capstone, [2026] | Series: Pebble maker baking | Audience: Ages 5–8 | Audience: Grades 2–3 | Summary: "A warm cookie is a special treat. Early and emergent readers can bake their own batch of sugar cookies topped with colorful sprinkles! Step-by-step instructions plus clear photos guide elementary children through this simple and sweet recipe that they (with a little adult assistance) can make themselves—and then enjoy!"—Provided by publisher.
Identifiers: LCCN 2024048982 (print) | LCCN 2024048983 (ebook) | ISBN 9798875224300 (hardcover) | ISBN 9798875224256 (paperback) | ISBN 9798875224263 (pdf) | ISBN 9798875224270 (epub) | ISBN 9798875224287 (kindle edition)
Subjects: LCSH: Cookies—Juvenile literature. | LCGFT: Cookbooks.
Classification: LCC TX772 .B645 2026 (print) | LCC TX772 (ebook) | DDC 641.86/54—dc23/eng/20241029
LC record available at https://lccn.loc.gov/2024048982
LC ebook record available at https://lccn.loc.gov/2024048983

Editorial Credits
Editor: Abby Cich; Designer: Heidi Thompson; Media Researcher: Jo Miller; Production Specialist: Tori Abraham

Image Credits
Capstone: Karen Dubke, front and back cover, 1, 8, 9, 12-17, 19, 21, 23; Shutterstock: PeopleImages.com - Yuri A, 7, Sandra Chia, 5, Vera Petrunina, 11

The publisher and the author shall not be liable for any damages allegedly arising from the information in this book, and they specifically disclaim any liability from the use or application of any of the contents of this book.

Any additional websites and resources referenced in this book are not maintained, authorized, or sponsored by Capstone. All product and company names are trademarks™ or registered® trademarks of their respective holders.

Printed and bound in China. 6274

TABLE OF CONTENTS

Simply Sweet... 4

Kitchen Tips 6

What You Need....................................... 8

What You Do 10

Take It Further 22

Glossary 24

About the Author 24

Words in **BOLD** are in the glossary.

SIMPLY SWEET

The first known cookie recipe was written 4,000 years ago. It was from modern-day Iran. Today, people all over the world eat cookies. Cookies can have frosting. They can be plain. But they are all yummy.

Get ready to bake your own tasty cookies!

KITCHEN TIPS

Stay safe and have fun with these tips.

- Have an adult helper nearby. Ask them to help with hot or sharp things.

- Read the recipe before you start. Get all your **ingredients** and tools.

- Wash your hands before you begin.

- Help clean up when you are done!

WHAT YOU NEED

INGREDIENTS

- 1/2 cup (113 grams) unsalted butter, room temperature

- 1/2 cup (99 g) white sugar

- 1/2 cup (106 g) brown sugar

- 1 egg

- 1 teaspoon (5 milliliters) vanilla **extract**

- 2 cups (240 g) flour

- 1/2 teaspoon (3 g) baking soda

- 1/2 teaspoon (3 g) salt

- sprinkles

TOOLS

- measuring cups and spoons
- large mixing bowl
- **hand mixer**
- medium mixing bowl
- mixing spoon
- 2 spoons
- small bowl
- 2 cookie sheets or baking sheets
- **flat spatula**
- cooling rack

WHAT YOU DO

STEP 1

Ask an adult to move one rack to the top of the oven. Put the other in the middle. Have the adult **preheat** the oven to 350°F (175°C).

STEP 2

Put the butter in the large bowl. Add the white and brown sugars. **Beat** with the hand mixer. Go 1 to 2 minutes. Stop when it looks fluffy and light brown.

Crack the egg into the bowl. Take out any shell with a spoon. Add the vanilla extract. Beat again. Go till the **mixture** is smooth.

STEP 3

Put the flour, baking soda, and salt into the medium bowl. Stir it with the mixing spoon.

Add half the flour mixture to the large bowl. Beat till you can't see flour. Repeat with the rest of the flour. Scrape the bowl with the spoon. Make sure there are no dry spots.

STEP 4

Use the 2 spoons to make 16 even balls of **dough**. Pour some sprinkles into the small bowl. Roll each ball in the sprinkles. Place 8 balls on each cookie sheet. Space the balls out evenly.

STEP 5

Ask the adult to put the cookies in the oven. One sheet will be on the top rack. One will be on the middle rack. Bake for 5 minutes. Then have the adult switch which racks the sheets are on. Bake for 5 to 7 minutes more.

Are the cookies a little brown on the edges?
Then they are done!

STEP 6

Let the cookies cool for 5 minutes. Then use the flat spatula to move them to the cooling rack. Enjoy cookies warm or cooled!

Keep extras in a zip-top bag for 1 week. Or freeze them. They will be good for 8 to 12 months.

TAKE IT FURTHER

Change up your cookie! Don't roll the dough in sprinkles. Add a topping. Try:

- chocolate chips
- candy-coated chocolates
- white sugar
- raisins
- crushed pretzels

GLOSSARY

beat (BEET)—to mix food by stirring in a fast circular motion

dough (DOH)—a mixture of flour and a liquid or other food (such as yeast, fat, or sugar) that is ready to be baked

extract (EK-strakt)—a liquid used for flavoring

flat spatula (FLAT SPACH-yoo-lah)—a utensil that is used to lift, turn, or flip food

hand mixer (HAND MIKS-uhr)—a handheld electric tool with two beaters that can turn quickly

ingredient (in-GREE-dee-uhnt)—a food that is put with other foods to make a recipe

mixture (MIKS-cher)—a mix of two or more ingredients

preheat (PREE-heet)—to heat an oven to a certain temperature before baking

ABOUT THE AUTHOR

Mari Bolte has been baking—and writing books about baking—since the beginning of time. (Well, it feels like that, anyway.) These days, she squeezes in loaves of no-knead bread and trays of sweet treats in between writing projects.